the sun
will
rise
again

Becca Reece

Copyright © 2024 by Rebecca Reece

All rights reserved. No part of this book may be reproduced or used in any manner without written permission of the copyright owner except for the use of quotations in a book review. For more information, address: mcpiper82@gmail.com

First paperback edition April 2024

Cover design by Rebecca Reece

ISBN 979-8-8836-8902-3 (paperback)

Independently published

the sun will rise again

For all those who have felt the great pains and loves of life and looking for a brighter tomorrow. Keep moving, my dear loves, it'll come soon enough.

Dear Authors
How do you do it?
How do you pick up your pen every single day?

How do you manage to write
Even though you're dealing with burn out

How can you continue to write
When your words make no sense

How can you record the words
While the world is barreling towards you

How can you write
When motivation has left you far behind

How can you write?
Oh God give me the strength

It's beautiful
The crows remark
Flying high above
Those snow capped mountains

It's gorgeous
The deer explain
Frolicking through
Those cold winter fields

It's breathtaking
The squirrels chitter
Climbing around
Those leafless trees

It's magical
The fox barks
Scrounging through
The abandoned burrows

The world awakes
Sparkling as the morning light shines
White blankets hold the beings in its grasps
Gray mist smother those proud mountains

I'm there
Covered like the rest of the world
But I can't move to shake off the cover
It holds me with those cold hands

It hurts
As a light so bright blinds me
I wish I could look away
But my body is frozen

This is torturous
I need to get back home
It would be warmer there
I would be able to eat some nice food

Where is everyone?
Why am I so alone?
Frozen to this concrete
I guess death really is lonely and cold after all

How I long
To stare forever
Into those eyes

Eyes azure as the sky
Reflecting perfect sunlight
Holding many secrets

Secrets I wish someday
You'll share with me
Though many already

Already you're more than perfect
Each day you dazzle
With magnificence you carry

Your eyes meet mine
My heart skips
I hold my breath
I wait for the butterflies

But they never come
They never do
I'm not anxious around you
You make me feel as myself

I want to spend
Every waking hour
With you beside me
For the rest of time

We're so close
Emotionally and physically
Our hands brush
A small smile crosses my lips

I just wish
Our love for one another
Wasn't as forbidden
As people claim

His face
Like a starry sky
His eyes
Reflected sweet kindness

His body
Always by my side
His hand
Forever in mine

His laugh
As music to my ears
His smile
Brightening up the darkest days

How I wish
That it wasn't
Just a distant memory
Too far from my grasps

How I wish
These ashes
Didn't continue pushing
Pushing me to keep going

Can't I just place my hands
Over my ringing ears
Blocking out the world
Just longing for his presence

Why do these ashes
Of my dear Love
Haunt me so
I just want him back

I talk
Seeking love
Finding only criticism

I remain silent
I won't say another thing
For everything I do
Just turns into a war

I just want affirmation
To say something
Not worrying about being torn down

Instead my words are shredded
Stripped to the bone
Rubbed raw
Only picking out the evil

Is anything I do
Good enough for you
Am I just the problem child

I guess I do nothing right
I am just a mistake after all
Walking a path of difference
A disappointment to the world

Soon I'll fade away
Into the deep abyss
To be forgotten
With all my problems

The heart is a fragile thing
It can shatter with a touch of pain
And it won't easily mend

I have shattered ones heart before
I was cruel to do so
It hurts to think

It makes me wonder though
Was it the right thing to do?
Did I do something wrong?

I shake and cry
As I think about it
Why am I cruel?

I want to fix this problem
And fix the heart
But I can't

I made the right decision
I need to fix me before continuing
Then maybe I can fix it

When she pulls out the candy
She can't take it anymore
She can't feel anything
She doesn't care anymore

When she takes a bite of it
It tastes so good
Its flavor stabs her tongue with feeling
It almost brings a smile to her face

Almost
The sensation always ends way too soon
And the numbness returns
So she eats another

And another
And another
Until there is no more
No more short lived happiness

My dear loves
There are too many of you to count
Your personalities very
From super sweet and kind
To cruel and thoughtless

We've been on many adventures
From the great skies full of dragons
To the great deep woods
Ending in great land of fire
They ended too quickly

We've been through too much
I've seen your struggles
Your hurts
I've seen you love
Seen you laugh

All of you are broken
From people running experiments on
To just trying to find a place to belong
But most of you didn't let that stop you
While others just let it consume

You guys have helped me
Helped me ride upon dragons
Helped me master magnificent powers
You've helped me deal with the hate
You've helped me live

Through you I was able to vent
I was able to share my true feelings
You made it so I could breathe
So I could be a different person then I was
So I could be loved

You all mean so much to me
I miss you all
This brain has aged
So I've forgotten some of your names
But you all have taught me so much
I love you all

Drag me through Hell
Tear me apart
Spit in my face
Trample me

I feel nothing
Your lies fly past
I can't hear them
All I see is you

You are perfect to me
You make me feel good
I just want to hold your hand
You've cast a spell upon me

Other people see it
They scream at my bloodied body
They try shaking sense into me
Nothing can get past my thick skull

Drag me through Hell
Leave me for dead
But I will follow you
Because I love you

Why do you hate me?
Was it something I did?
What can I do to change?
Should I work harder?

Questions asked
Only answer
We don't hate you
How could you think that?

Why do they lie?
Why do they criticize,
Every little thing I do
Never a good job

I try everything
I do the dirty work
I sacrifice my happiness for theirs
Will nothing please them?

I don't want trouble
Our relationship is good, right?
We have fun
Everything is fine

But why are you quiet?
Why do you ignore me?
Barely say a word to me?
Only to say I'm a failure

Thank you
I guess that's what I really am
I can't do anything
Without you telling me everything I did wrong

Maybe I should melt away
End my life
Funny thing is
I can't even do that

There is no end in goodbye
So why do we think of them as the final chapter
Why do we use it to signify the ending climax
In one way there is no end

Why do we spend time with others
Only to have them depart from you
What's the point of friendships
Only to have them crumble at a single word

There seems to be no reason
To this thing people call relationships
They all end
We all say farewell

Yes, everything ceases
But this thing called companionship
It helps us grow
Helps us continue going

But we say so long
There is no point to growth
If you bond with someone on such deep levels
Only to have them ripped from you

But what would a person do
Without the deep connections
It hurts on the most intense levels
To watch those people leave

Haven't I told you before
There is no end in goodbye
We will see those dear people again
We just don't know when

Goodbyes are what keep us going
It pushes us
Drags us forward with such haste
Tells us we will see them again

Yes, they are cruel
I hate them with every ounce of my being
It's just a new chapter with new characters
Possibly a cameo of the old

Have you felt alone?
Have you felt the pain eat away at your soul?
Have you longed for revenge?
Have you lost everything?

Have you screamed as your soul was swallowed?
Have you seen the people dear to you leave?
Have you sat in the dark feeling useless?
Have you cried as your father yelled?

Have you felt as if there is no purpose in life?
Have you felt your life fade before your eyes?
Have you taken the life of someone close to you?
Have you lost your mind and hope?

Have you sought to touch the stars?
Have you dreamed an impossible dream?
Have you fought for what you believe?
Have you seen miracles before your eyes?

Have you seen those lost become found?
Have you reached a hand out to the ones wallowing in pain?
Have you smiled at the ones everyone ignores?
Have you clung to hope as the world crashes around?

When I look at you
I know I can not have you
Your amazing smile
Your cute laugh
Your stupid jokes
Your spunky spirit
I wish those things could be mine
To cherish
But they're not
And they'll never be
But I can still wish
And smile at you
Because maybe we can defy destiny
And you'll be mine
And I'll be yours

Some days seem like a dream
They pass before your eyes
Faster than lightning
You move in fluid motion
One with the crowd
Sometimes you have no idea what has happened
Other times you remember in full detail
You wish to break free
You wish to wake up
But sometimes you are awake
And your dream is a nightmare of reality

She stood
Her back to the wind
Overlooking a green valley
It had taken her awhile to get there
She had climbed many a mountain
Forded many a stream
Crossed many a valley
She now stood looking how far she'd come
She could now relax
Now put up her feet
Now she was home
She had made it

In a time of no time
A land far but near
Trembled and fell
No one saw it coming
No one saw it happening
Except for the poor farm boy
And the young merchant girl
They were the only ones
They'll always be the only ones

I feel so far away
Far away from this world
Far away from the ones I love

What is making me feel this way?
Why do I dread to see anyone?
Why do I ache when I'm with them?

I stare in the mirror
Hating myself for everything
Hating the way I interact with anyone

I fall to my knees, shaking
I just want to give up
I just want people to leave me alone

I feel the darkness swallow me
It almost feels good
It almost makes me happy

But the happiness lasts for seconds
There is no way out
There is no more freedom

There is no chance of escape
No form of rescue
No form of anything, just darkness

But a hand grasps mine
Holding on tightly
Holding as if I'm slipping

The hand pulls me out of the darkness
Into a light so bright
Into something beautiful

The darkness still lurks
Waiting for me to slip

Waiting for me to give up

But I won't
Because I'm stronger than it
Because I'm a fighter

I think about death
More than normal people
It sounds so peaceful
Yet so terrifying

That's what makes it intriguing
It's so cold
Yet so warm
I want to crawl into its embrace

Others say that's wrong
While some say go for it
But you wouldn't have to worry
About Death hurting you, right?

I feel as if Death is lonely
Just like I am
If I join it
Then we'd be together

Death is kind
But it can be cruel
It doesn't like it
But cruel is necessary at times

Why can't Death come to take me?
I can't stand being alive
Life is hard
Death seems softer

Death, I plead
Come with haste
I'm tired
I can't do anymore

```
I want to get lost forever with you
I want to feel you for eternity
I want to remove your mask

Why won't you hold me
Why won't you recognize me as something more
Why won't you realize I love you
```

Life is beautiful
But it hurts me
Oh the pain
Oh the horror
Wait!
What was that?
Did you just say you loved me?
Lies!
If you loved me
Then why did you yell at me?
Why did you say those words?

Life is amazing
But it burns me
Oh the heat
Oh the scars
Wait!
What was that?
Did you just hit me?
Why?
What have I done to you?
I stuck with you to the end

Life is a treasure
But it breaks me
Oh the damage
Oh the fractures
Wait!
What was that?
Did you just say you were sorry?
Lies!
If you're sorry
Why do you keep hurting me?
Why do you ignore me?

Life is astonishing
But it kills me
Oh the destruction

Oh the annihilation
Wait?
Did I forgive you?
No, I didn't
Then I forgive you
You have done me wrong
But I still love you
Do you still love me?

A question most often asked
Why're you so happy?
How do you smile
While your world crashes down around

I always turn
A small smile playing on my lips
I tell them
It's the little things

It's the little sparrow
Fluffing itself in the puddle
While the water reflects
Reflects the warm sunshine

It's the warm feeling
Coffee gives you
As you gently sip
While you slowly awake to the world

It's the little conversations
With the someone you care about the most
Late into the night
Unaware of time passing

It's the overjoyed dog
Who greets you every morning
Tail wagging
While a toy hangs from his mouth

It's the gentle snow
Falling peacefully on the cold ground
As you walk at night
Warm air escaping your lungs

It's a whisper
So soft and mild
Of a voice uttering
You're not alone

Loneliness
Something no one wants to experience
Something that crushes ones soul
That brings people to a painful end

It is like a battle
Raging on around you
Roaring in your ears
But you're the dead man everyone tramples over, ignoring
You're the soldier left behind because you're too weak

It is like a ball
People dancing past you, laughing
Joyfulness all around you
But everyone looks past you
Everyone picks the people beside and around you

It is a quiet room
Silence swallowing your soul
Faint noises of people having fun nearby
But you're laying in your bed, tears in your eyes
Wanting to be apart of the fun but no one knows you

A scaly head turned upwards
Staring at the swirling storm of stars above
A tear trickled out of those jade eyes
Thinking of what was to come
A mournful howl escaped its mouth

A gentle hand rested on its shoulder
Calming the shaking beast
A soft voice whispered to it
Whispering not to fear
To have peace

The mythical beast raised its head
Spreading its giant black wings
Leaped into the smoky air
Soaring higher and higher
Into the starry storm

The creature soon disappeared
Being sucked into the eye of the storm
To never be seen again

Standing on the ridge
Wind blowing her tousled hair
Listening to the Canaries sing their cheerful songs
Smelling the fallen birch and spruce

Watching the crystal waves below lap against the shore
Seeing an occasional dolphin break the water's surface
In a joyous jump

Looking over the bay at the quiet town
The sun lying lazily over it
Silvery smoke being whisked away into the blue sky

How she wished to capture the beauty
How she wished she could put it in a little bottle
And take it with her always
How she wished to stay there forever

But she had to head back
Back to the real world
And away from that beautiful fantasy

She was handed the world
But she turned it down
She wanted just to live
And to not have a crown

Her father insisted
And forced the weight upon her
She could not refuse
So there was no need for a confer

A few years later
Her father passed on
In the war that killed most
The world was almost gone

She looked over the land
Tears streaming down
It was then she realized
That she was born to have the crown

Before I met you, I was insane
I had an obscure way of thinking
I thought life was all about surviving
Putting one foot in front of the other
Then you came along
Showed me that life was so much more
You added a bit more insanity to my life
You made me think in a more obscure way
You helped me survive the rocky road of life
Even when I stumbled and couldn't go on
I would close my eyes and think of you
Then I would get up and see you standing there
Arms open

Heart flutters
Why must it do that
Every time a thought of you
Occurs in my brain

Why is it
When my eyes
Fall upon you
I can't breathe

My stomach twists
When I read
A message you kindly sent
That brings a smile

I'm in pain
You're splendid
Absolutely stunning
But never mine

Shattered windows
Burnt walls
Trampled lilies
Fallen forests

All so bleak
Such a sad sight
But
Look closely

Growing grasses
Climbing ivy
Dancing Dandelions
Singing birds

You're in pain
I know you smile
Laugh boisterously
Applying a brave expression

You're hidden beneath layers
A soft coating of protection
So no one can see your weakness
Though I do

I see the battle
The battle waged behind those eyes
Those eyes so sad
It wearing you down

No one else sees
No one else seems to care
I care
Please let me help

Let me take the burden you carry
None should have to bare it alone
You aren't weak
In fact you're stronger than me

I want you to know
You aren't alone
I'm here
Holding you through this nightmare

I won't be like you
Those words
So full of confidence
Knowing I won't be like you
But I just sit
I don't do anything about the scars
I let the hurt swallow me
Letting the pain consume my thoughts
Until I'm just like you

The past returns
Rises from the ashes of old
Threatening to smite out
All the good that has sprung anew

All the work put forth
To change the course of the future
Shattered at one's feet
From just a choice

He used to get excited when the phone rang
When the numbers came
Thrilled to be able to help others
To stop horrible things from happening

But as time went on
As people died
As criminals got away
As friends got hurt

He began to lose hope
This was taking everything from him
His lover
His friends

He became truly alone
Just him and the numbers
The numbers that never stopped
While all he could do was watch

Watch as the world burned
He didn't even try anymore
He needed someone to help
Someone with the skills to intervene

Closing in
The forest
Swallowing whole
The road

Life springing
From death
Man's creation
To dust

Tall pines
Little ferns
Taking breathe
Into lungs

No more road
Just remanence
The forest
Closing in

Only two years
So much has changed
Life was changed
For the better, right

Change is good
For normal people
Going from state to state
Having to put new roots down

Only for two years
The chemical unbalance
Threw my mind into a pit
Too far to climb out

The darkness swallowed me
There was no focus on studies
For it vanished without a goodbye
I was alone

People go about their day
Not caring
Not noticing
Just focusing on themselves

People pass me all the time
In the halls
In the classroom
They sometimes smile
Sometimes ignore

I just stay to myself
Smiling, showing happiness
When someone talks to me
Blocking out the quietness
And the void
Showing that I'm not actually breaking

Then when I'm alone
The pain slowly crawls back
The void swallows me
Fear creeps in
Chomping on my last bit of hope
Anxiety crashes in like a wrecking ball
That's when the loneliness strikes

Sitting at my desk
Looking out the window
Feeling hollow
I want to cry
I want to somehow let it out
But there's nothing there
I'm losing interest in the things I love
I need to distract myself

Distracting doesn't work anymore
I find myself being drawn to the window
More and more so

The gray clouds hanging low
The droplets of water dripping down the glass
Like tears
I long to sit on the ledge of it
I want to feel the wind in my face
I want to be inside those solemn clouds

I just want to feel something
I just want to smile
Without having to force it
I want to laugh freely
I want to know what it feels like,
To go to bed
And not lie in bed questioning life
I want to stop hating myself
I wish the void would leave
I wish I could just breathe freely

I see you everyday
A fine friend
Wishing we could be more
But knowing it will never happen
Knowing that a destiny will never cross again
Knowing that you were meant for someone else
Someone special
Someone who will make you smile everyday
Someone who you keeps you up thinking
I wish to be that someone
But I know that someone isn't me

She stood by her own grave
Nunchucks hung on her belt
Seeing the stains of blood
That marked the icy stone

A chilly wind swirled around her
Whispers of her past flowed near her ears
A silent tear rolled down her broken face
Falling to ground like a rolling boulder

Come back
A voice called a distance away
You are strong
Don't fall into this trap

She raised her head at the black sky
The tears gone
She exhaled stale air
That had been held onto too long

She used a torn hand to wipe away the red from the stone
Removing that name
That name she was given from hate
It was time to start anew
And say goodbye to the old

We step away
To part to different worlds
My hand still grasped in yours
Not wanting to let go

We're forced apart by destiny
It hurts
I can't live alone
I can't live without you

Every second away from you kills my soul
I feel empty
I can't breath
I cry myself to sleep

And then when I see you again
My heart shatters
My chest closes up
And I'm blown away

I don't know how to respond
I shake
You're just so wonderful
I just want to hold and kiss you

But I can't
I can't do any of that
I'm too scared
I feel as if I'd mess everything up

Eyes focused on distant waters
Watching it churn
Wild waves crashing upon broken shores
Which were once whole

No one seems to notice
Their eyes trained on something bigger
They have no need to focus
On those torn up beaten shores

The shore however
It's crumbling
It's existence barely noticeable
No way of returning to its past state

That burning desire
Fire igniting the soul
Consuming every sense of stability
As my eyes fall upon you

I hunger to be with you
For your arms around me
Holding me as the world burns
As it all fades away to darkness

But that's just it
Darkness
The unwelcoming touch of loneliness
Choking out any sense of feeling

You were never there
Never desiring me
Never wanting to spend eternity with
I was just a pawn

Just an experiment
Something needing fixing
Your intentions were good
But you did more harm

Am I that unloveable
That unattractive
No more than a friend
Romantics never on your mind

He always smiled
He was always joyful
He never grew impatient

He would tease me relentlessly
I don't remember seeing a frown on that face
Only when he was deep in thought

All that changed
When I had to go and die
He was supposed to be the one to die young

He become irritable
Anger seemed to consume him
Rage and pain seemed to seep into his soul

That bright soul became clouded by darkness
I wasn't sure if he sought revenge
Or sought rest for his soul

He never smiled anymore
Except when he killed someone
But it wasn't a true smile

Was this all my fault?
Was it I who caused this?
Did I stop his smile?

I guess I'll ask him when he joins me
It won't be long
He's on his way now

We were assassins, the both of us.
We served nobody, except her.
We killed for her without hesitation.
We never questioned her, why should we?
We obeyed her every word and followed her every order.
We would have served her till our dying breath.
We now look back and wonder,
Why did we do what we did?
Why did we follow her?

Playing quietly in my room
With a feeling of contentment
Not knowing I did anything wrong
Thundering footsteps up the stairs

Confusion as they ran in
Started yelling
I was trapped
No way out

Wall pressed into my back
I didn't feel it
So much noise
What are they even saying?

Crumpling into ball
Eardrums bursting
I can't hear myself think
MAKE IT STOP

What did I do?
Did I deserve this?
Probably
I was a failure after all

"I'm sorry"
Repeated constantly
No one listened
Roaring all around

Alone
That's how I've always ended
I've had friends
I've had love

All my life
Show and Tell
"Oh there goes that boy"
They'd point and laugh

My best friend was among them
Laughing right along
All eyes on me
Who am I?

I had my siblings
They loved me
We were family
Then it was just my sister

My guy best friend
We did everything
I had him for life
Well, the rest of his life

I wasn't there
He passed alone
Overworked to the maximum
Where was I?

She was beautiful
Woman of my dreams
She sprinkled a bit of spice
In my very dull life

She had a heart for others
Her smile lit up darkness
She was going to be my wife

The rest of my life would be with her

Another man swept her off her feet
He was beyond attractive
I could not compare
He was cruel though

But then again, aren't we all
He didn't treat her right
He kept pretending he'd changed
He stole her from me

Alone
That's how it always has been
Life just dragged that in my face
Giving me false hope

The world darkening
Closing in
That sinking feeling
Settling in

Time flying by
Making friends anew
Not having to worry
Of those lurking shadows

Or so you thought
The shadows great
Too powerful to withstand
Creep back in

Alone again
In the dark
Makes you wonder
Is it meant to be

She knew she could be anything
Anything her heart desired
Yet she was nothing
Barely a whisper in the morning breeze

She tried hard to become great
There was always someone greater
Their greatness clouded her mind
She gave up

She sat alone
Eyes fixed on the wall
Not a penny to her name
Name unknown to all

Her fight was gone
They won again
In the end
She'll just fade away

It's that feeling again
Of losing someone so dear
Someone you've known
At least thought so

The fun times spent
Caring nothing of time
Laughing so joyously
Never wanting to leave

Now you yearn to leave
Can't bear a moment more
The fun is gone
Only pain remains

You wonder why
Why could they do that
How could they hate you
What happened

With questions unanswered
You walk away
Defeated and alone
Friendship forever gone

It's too dark
Eyes can't make out
Can't bring air in
Struggling to take a step

Rocks and stumps spring up
Feet stumbling
Pain shooting through the soul
I can't breathe

Hope no more
Being swallowed whole
Body battered
All light gone

Or so thought
Though quite dim
A small flame flickered
Pulling one forward

Hope reignited
Though just a spark
Encourages the broken
To drag those sorry legs

Look up
At the passing clouds
The beauty of the heavens
A bird soaring high above

Look forward
At the blowing leaves
The swaying trees
A deer frolicking by

Look down
At the blooming tulips
The fragrant wildflowers
A beetle skittering around

Do you think
All such details
Placed for a reason
For one to enjoy

We are all ships on an ocean
We are all boats on a lake
Usually the water is calm
And we sail smoothly without trouble
But when storms rise up
We rock and sway
We are pelted with rain and hail
Lightning flashes
Thunder rumbles
And wind rips at our sails
Some ships sink below the waves
They sink because they gave up
But we stay afloat
Our sails torn and masts fallen
And our hulls full of holes
We could have given up like the others
But we persevered
We came through
Because we are strong

The end… or is it?
Does it end?
Or is it only beginning?
The beginning of something new
The beginning of a new outlook

Forward

Hello all! I just wanted to thank you for going through and reading my thoughts and stories thrown into groups of words we call poems. I know some may have been a bit hard to swallow, but that's life sometimes. I hope you were able to learn something and come out with a new outlook of life. I also hope you know that you aren't alone! You never are! Thank you all again.
Also a special thanks to all my family and friends who have supported me during this. You guys mean the world to me.

Made in the USA
Middletown, DE
25 April 2024